Walk in Their Shoes

Walk in Their Shoes

A Day in the School Life of an Spld student

Edwina Cole

Barrington Stoke

Published in 2004 in Great Britain by
Barrington Stoke Ltd, Sandeman House, Trunk's Close,
55 High Street, Edinburgh EH1 1SR
www.barringtonstoke.co.uk

ISBN 1-84299-162-0

Edited by Julia Rowlandson
Illustrations by Stuart Boyde
Typeset by GreenGate Publishing Services, Tonbridge, Kent
Printed in Great Britain by The Cromwell Press

Contents

I couldn't understand why he couldn't do the work I had set.

He was exceptionally able and I had high expectations …

but

he was frustrated

and I was disappointed.

Then he started to talk …

I listened, and I, the teacher began to learn from my pupil.

It was the defining moment in my teaching career.

Introduction

Education is about teaching and learning. Traditionally, the teacher teaches and the pupil listens and learns. For many this system works, but for others it becomes a nightmare of missed opportunities where the teacher and the pupil seem to be on different planets.

When Maslow put forward his hierarchy of human needs in 1954, he divided them into two distinct groups: deficiency needs and growth needs. When we look at the first four levels, the deficiency needs, in relation to students with specific learning difficulties, it is immediately apparent that if we fail to take these needs into account, it compounds their individual problems. The order of satisfying these needs is important, and time and again students indicate either verbally or by their actions, that they need their physical needs of hunger, thirst and comfort met first. This is followed by a need to feel secure and then to be accepted by others. The need to achieve, and to gain approval and recognition, is then acknowledged. It is only when these deficiency needs have been met that individuals can move on to the growth need of knowing and understanding, which is where teachers and students meet.

Nowadays, we are beginning to understand that learning and teaching styles are the keys to unlocking the potential that lurks in every student. We all know of people who look back on their schooling with a mixture of sadness, disappointment and not a little resentment because for them the system did not work. Perhaps some of their basic deficiency needs were not met, perhaps they never discovered the ways in which they could learn most effectively, and their teachers, in the main, were not open to adapting their teaching to accommodate varying learning needs.

"Unconditional helping relationships form the foundation of unconditional schools. The students who most need these relationships are those who most challenge their teachers."

[David Lloyd – 2001 Unconditional schools, Youth of Promise.]

It is vital that schools adopt a team approach to helping these students. Everyone who is involved with them should stop and listen and learn from what they say and do, passing on what works and what does not. If this does not happen, the students are repeatedly getting caught up in the same scenario.

Teachers, by definition, are successful learners, and the best of them never stop learning, experimenting and taking risks. They need to be constantly searching for the best way to explain something to the student who learns in a different way.

Of course, in today's educational climate there are huge pressures on both teachers and learners. Too few teachers have the time and opportunity to work one-to-one with students and inclusion policies mean that those with specific learning needs are more and more likely to find themselves learning in larger groups.

The purpose of this book is to eavesdrop on the students, and to listen to what they say about their school experiences. It is not a scientific survey, but a series of observations recorded in the hope that it may inform and ease the path to inclusion. The information was gathered via a questionnaire that was sent to a variety of schools, and members of staff, with whom the students felt at ease, carried out the interviews. For the teacher in the classroom it may offer some insights into the way it really is for these young people, and for some of them at least, point to a different way of responding and teaching to make learning more enjoyable. For the student in school it may be comforting to discover that they are not as isolated as they thought and that others share their experiences and think in a similar way.

The five chapters in the book relate to five specific learning difficulties. These are ADHD, Asperger's Syndrome, dyslexia, dyspraxia and speech and language difficulties. Readers may find it helpful to refer to the following short definitions. Further information is given in the chapters that follow.

ADHD

This stands for Attention Deficit Hyperactivity Disorder. Poor attention, distractibility and impulsivity are the hallmarks of these students. They are overactive and unable to inhibit their behaviour. Calling out, interrupting and off task behaviour can alienate them from their peers and teachers.

It is thought that 30% of those with dyslexia or a conduct disorder will experience problems with attention, making it difficult to concentrate on any job, activity or lesson. Many more boys than girls are affected and they have more difficulty acquiring self-management skills than others.

Asperger's syndrome

Asperger's syndrome is generally considered to be on the 'autistic spectrum'. Students may have problems with communication, social interaction and imagination. There may be obsessional and ritualistic behaviours and resistance to change. Pupils are unable to see life from another's point of view. They have extreme difficulty transferring skills learnt in one situation to another.

Dyslexia

The British Dyslexia Association offers the following definition:

"Dyslexia is best described as a combination of abilities and difficulties which affect the learning process in one or more of the following: reading, spelling, writing and sometimes numeracy and/or language. Accompanying weaknesses may be identified in the following areas: speed of processing, short-term memory, sequencing, auditory and/or visual perception, spoken language and motor skills."

Dyspraxia

Dyspraxia describes a range of perceptuo-motor difficulties. Particular problem areas are difficulty in the planning and co-ordination of motor tasks affecting self-help skills, fine motor skills such as handwriting, drawing, cutting with scissors and using a ruler. Gross motor skills result in difficulties in PE, problems with spatial tasks and general clumsiness, untidiness and disorganisation. Speech can appear disorganised due to problems with planning what to say and then co-ordinating the actual words. A difficulty in understanding or following rules can further affect social interaction.

Speech and language difficulties

These can be very diverse, describing a range of difficulties in the acquisition of language and communication. Students can have specific problems in one area only or a mixture of problems in several areas. Some will have difficulty with expressive language, finding the words and constructing the sentences to say what they want. Whilst others have trouble with receptive language which affects their learning and causes problems with social interaction.

Students with articulation problems were not interviewed for this book.

Ultimately, if this book opens discussion, offers explanations or reassures then it has achieved its objective. It may be helpful to think about students as having specific learning needs or differences rather than difficulties. This is an important distinction, since difficulty implies a problem. Meeting someone's needs, on the other hand, may be simpler, cheaper and certainly less costly in terms of disillusionment and disappointment.

In Haim Ginott's famous words from his book, *"Between Teacher and Child"* 1972:

As a teacher I possess tremendous power to make a child's life miserable or joyous.

I can be a tool of torture or an instrument of inspiration.

I can humiliate or humor, hurt or heal.

In all situations, it is my response that decides whether a crisis will be escalated or de-escalated, and a child humanized or de-humanized.

Acknowledgements

I wish to thank all those students and colleagues who have taught me and inspired me, and especially those at Stanbridge Earls School, Romsey, Hampshire.

Thanks are also due to those students who have directly contributed to this book.

Robert Barlow
Jake Bennett
Stuart Boyde, who provided
  the illustrations as well
Martin Cahow
Ryan Claire
Chris Davenport
Sam Giddings
Jade Harris
Edward Hood
Ben Manners

Luke Matthews
Anna Millis
Edward O'Callaghan
Daniel O'Leary
Loreilei Rogers
Angus Rogers
Fergus Rogers
Ben Sharkey
Sam Stinner
Luke Williams
Daniel Winter

I should also like to acknowledge the contributions of those many students who gave their views, but wished not to be named.

Finally, I would thank my family and friends for their support, encouragement and initial proofreading!

Edwina Cole
January 2004

ADHD

We are still grappling with the concept of ADHD, a difficulty that encompasses one or many of the following: impulsivity, inattentiveness, hyperactivity, poor behaviour and inconsistent achievement. There cannot be a school in the country that is not struggling to understand and deal with pupils who exhibit these problems. Yet there is continued disagreement over diagnosis and treatment. Against this background, students who fall into this category give themselves, their families and their schools considerable cause for concern.

It is not yet clear whether there is a deficit in psychological processes related to attention, or indeed if there is another cause. What is known is that more boys than girls are affected, and a figure of between 3% and 6% is usually given.

In school, these students present as restless and impulsive. They will have poor concentration/attention spans and probably exhibit poor visual or auditory memory. Difficulties are not confined to the school situation, and parents report similar behaviours at home. Not surprisingly, coupled with this, is often an uneven pattern of attainment.

One of the most contentious issues is whether these students should be prescribed medication in order to give those who care for them and those who teach them a 'window of time' in which to do so.

Attitudes vary as to what constitutes a diagnosis, which may lead to the administration of such stimulants as Ritalin. The long-term effects of this drug are still being investigated and some young people have reservations about taking it. They cite various side effects as having a detrimental effect on their appetite and sleep patterns. However, it is clear that for some students medication, at least in the short term, is helpful and in some cases can make a student's life in school more tolerable both for them and for their teachers. In an extreme case, it can also be the key factor in preventing exclusion.

Starting the day

Students in this group focus their thinking about the day ahead on the lessons that they have, and the reactions that different lessons and different teachers may provoke. They do tend to reflect on the previous day and any unresolved issues that remain.

"If I am in the middle of a quarrel I feel scared, really scared and angry and often nervous about what will happen next."

They often have a heightened sense of justice and will pursue a cause relentlessly, demanding detailed explanations of why a particular course of action has been taken.

They find it hard to get up in the morning. *"I'm always late!"* But they organise their own uniform and equipment. Sometimes, they even develop their own strategies for making life easier.

"I normally put my books by the door as I am very forgetful."

They don't like the uniform very much. This is not because it's uncomfortable, but because *"it's not my choice"*, and because of the way the tie can be used. *"They can grab you by the tie and it gets really tight."* The use of *'they'* often describes actions they may well carry out themselves.

Some of these students are very bright. They are often hyper-vigilant, taking in every peripheral detail. They can often predict what may happen, and will think about ways in which they can defend themselves or avoid certain situations altogether.

Going to school

The school day does not seem to present any particular problems, but it is regarded as a bit of a chore. Time and time again, one senses disinterest and reluctance. *"I just don't look forward to it."* Perhaps, this may be because they know that they will inevitably get involved in some situations involving conflict and misunderstanding.

Starting the school day

For most students the day begins with Tutor/Form time, which is an opportunity for classmates to meet, and for the tutor to take the register. It is not a lesson as such, and therefore ADHD students do not consider it to be a very important part of the day.

"What's tutor time? Oh yes, we all sit down and do register and if you are late you are marked L!" "I didn't get on with my tutor due to a personality clash. The only thing she went on and on about was that my bag was a mess."

It is very difficult for these students to sit still and listen, particularly if they are not interested in what is being said and they cannot see the point of an activity. They need to understand that it is relevant to them, but frequently fail to engage their attention. This seems to happen most often during assembly time.

"We usually have to listen to comments on being good and being told off. I find it hard to sit still. I fidget or daydream."

"If I am with people I don't know I'm good, but when I am with my friends, if it's extra boring, I talk."

Teachers

It is clear that many teachers find these students particularly difficult to work with, perhaps because their behaviour can be unpredictable and is often disruptive to the class. It is also clear that the students themselves want to get it right, but it does take them time to settle down in lessons and it does matter who they sit next to.

"If I sit next to … who is also ADHD we seem to get into trouble."

"I have problems when I sit next to bad, not well behaved people. I try to be good but if the lessons are boring I talk to my friends."

The whole issue of teaching and learning styles is of tremendous importance for all students, but particularly so for those who find it so difficult to settle and to concentrate. It is difficult for them to just listen or look for long periods of time. They need to do things, and the teachers who connect best with this group are those who introduce a variety of activities into their lessons so that there are fewer opportunities for boredom to set in. The teacher is the key to successful learning, and students are quick to recognise what they need. They are equally disparaging about those who, perhaps unknowingly, make learning almost impossible because of inflexible teaching methods.

The best teachers are the best because *"I know where I stand with them. They are quite strict but fun."*

"She's funny, active, she likes doing things. She makes it interesting and exciting and does not say things over and over again."

Clearly, over-learning for ADHD students is irritating and unnecessary. They want to move on.

There are some heart-breaking examples of teachers and learners who inhabit different worlds.

"They just shout at me and send me out. They don't talk or give me a chance to explain."

"They want me to do things the moment they say. I will do them but I'm not ready when they say."

"If you say hello she's not interested and walks off. She makes the lessons boring and is extra strict. She wants to get you told off."

"The worst crime is to be boring."

The language that teachers use is a vital component in successful learning. Some students get lost in lessons because *"teachers use complicated grown-up language. Some explain it, but lots don't"*.

So many ADHD students clearly feel frustrated and misunderstood. Most of them really want to learn, but find that the systems in many schools simply don't make allowances for their needs. There is also a feeling that they are entitled to a better deal.

"If they make an effort with me, I will make an effort with them."

"I can't stop myself calling out."

What emerges from this is that, in the eyes of ADHD pupils, fewer teachers seem willing or able to make an effort to understand them. The main reason for this is probably because of the damaging effect their pattern of behaviour has on a whole class's learning. Sending these students out of lessons is counter-productive and simply reinforces their belief that the school cannot cope with them, and that they cannot cope with the school. However, being pro-active and asking them to do an errand for you, removes them from the classroom and can diffuse a potentially explosive incident, channelling the pupil's mental and physical energy in another direction without lowering their self-esteem.

Following a timetable

Timetables underpin the day's activities and most students view them as helpful. They also have views on what they would like to see on them.

"I'd like to have a good subject at the beginning and end of each day."

The routines that timetables impose can be useful because *"I'm not good with change. I get confused"*. They can also influence the attitude to certain lessons in advance.

"I arrive on time for the lessons that I like, but I get distracted on the way to the others."

It is interesting to think about the way we expect students to move between lessons. Some actually have a long way to go if they are on a large campus, and although it does provide a physical break, it can also break concentration, tempt ADHD students into off task activities and be a source of irritation.

"I don't like moving when I'm in the middle of a good subject or if I'm in the middle of a sentence because I want to finish it and normally you don't get time to."

It also leaves some students vulnerable to the ever-present problem of losing equipment or leaving things behind.

"I do sometimes leave my bag behind, but NOT on purpose."

Most students do not like to be parted from their possessions, however regularly they seem to lose things or leave them behind. It is probably as frustrating for them as it is for their teachers!

Reading aloud

This is not viewed with the same horror that other students express. Perhaps this is because it is a 'doing activity' and ADHD students tend to have a 'have a go' mentality. They can see it as an opportunity for showing what they can do rather than exposing yet another weakness.

In general, students don't understand the teacher's obsession with reading aloud because *"it sounds weird"* but they accept it as part of normal classroom practice and when asked whether they liked it or not the majority replied, *"I don't mind"*.

Break-times

Break-times are the opportunity for all students to let off steam and to relax. For ADHD students they can also act as a safety valve, providing an essential break between the formal and informal parts of the day. There-fore, it is often counter-productive to withdraw students from break-time as a punishment as you deprive them of the opportunity to let off steam and possibly exacerbate problems later in the day. They enjoy the chance to be with friends, to be active, to run around and to play football, but some like to be in control.

"I want to organise the games. Everyone starts shouting and talking and I want to shout, 'Stop it!' I want to tell them how to play."

Perhaps this is one of the major problems. In lessons, they have to toe the line, but in break-time they have the opportunity to tell others what to do and this can result in conflict. *"I remember arguments and gangs. I was usu-ally on top."* As the day progresses, incidents and irritations combine together to produce explosive situations over which they have no control. This is compounded by their natural impulsivity to say and do things without thinking, which often lead them to initiate activities with no thought for the eventual outcome. They appear to have little realisation of when a joke has gone too far but are the first to lose control if they are slighted.

Just as they have certain expectations of themselves, they also have expectations of others and when they fall short, will openly express their displeasure, with little regard for the other person's feelings.

"There is a gross boy who puts his face in his food and eats like a cat off his plate and that isn't good table manners."

Homework

Students in general dislike homework, but for this group it is particularly difficult.

"It is the worst part of school life."

Having coped all day at school in formal and restrictive situations they look forward to the end of the day and the chance to do what they like, but then homework comes along with its huge organisational load.

"I hate it because it takes up all the time you have after school."

Despite this, there is a general feeling that there is a reason for it.

"It is to remind you of what you did in the lesson." "It makes you clever!"

No subject emerges as being particularly enjoyed for homework, although on occasions when students have Art or PE work to do, this is less painful. Homework causes arguments for all sorts of reasons.

"They keep reminding me to do it." "I leave everything to the last moment and then everyone gets cross." "When my dad is doing Maths with us he says it over and over again and it gets really annoying."

For those who have concentration problems, homework comes at precisely the wrong time! It is asking a lot of anyone to do the one thing they find most difficult - to concentrate at the end of what may have been a hard and stressful day. It is, of course important that they should keep up with the work they need to do, but is it possible for staff to be more creative when setting homework tasks? More doing and less thinking and reading?

Examinations

Examinations pose the greatest test of concentration. For an extended period of time students are expected to sit and concentrate in order to demonstrate the breadth and depth of their learning. They can come as a shock to those who have been used to help and support.

"Are they tests? I sort of like them but I hate SATS."

"I don't look forward to them, but I have to get on with them."

The indignant question, *"How can I sit in there for an hour?"* is often resolved by the element of fear exams bring with them. This appears to check their hyperactive inclinations.

For some, the only salvation is the concession of short breaks, so that they can use maximum concentration for the time they actually spend in front of the exam paper. For others, the concession of a prompt can be helpful to keep them on track. Preparation for exams is vital, especially for those who race impulsively through the paper and then have time to kill at the end.

Some students simply walk out when they have done as much as they can. *"No point in staying in there."* They need to be taught to read the question more than once and then to have thinking time before they start to write. They should be taught to carry out a simple proof-reading strategy before declaring they have finished.

Social interaction – bullying

There is some intolerance amongst these students who cannot cope with others whose standards are clearly lower than their own. PE causes problems in that they find turn taking genuinely hard and are reluctant to be part of a team which may contain 'losers'.

They do, however, thrive as part of a crowd, although instances of teasing and, in some cases bullying, were reported.

"Some people use horrible words to others. Giraffe, big teeth, and spotty."

They are reluctant to admit to being victims of others, but sometimes tell of individual instances.

"I had loads of people trying to chase and hurt me."

They can also be bullies themselves, taking out their frustrations on others who are weaker than they are.

The end of the day brings homework, TV and other activities but many of these students like some time on their own. Maybe the reason for this is not too hard to find. *"I just need some time out."*

Confiding in friends and family comes easily to some, but not to others.

"I can definitely tell Mum my secrets, all the time."

"I won't say anything, no, not even if they ask me. I just say fine. I could but I don't."

Friends are very important.

"We were friends but for six weeks we have got on extra well and have been chilling together."

"I feel safe with my friends. I know I can tell them things I couldn't say to other people."

Bedtime

Going to bed and then to sleep may not a problem for those who are physically tired having expended extra energy during the day but for some it is a problem relaxing enough to go to sleep. When they are tired they can become extra silly and over excited.

Escaping into a secret world may be one way to deal with problems.

"I remember my teacher telling me a sad story about going to Heaven and I picture short yellow grass and a massive clear blue lake with a little circle of trees in the middle. I think of exploring with friends in a boat and then going into trees and making a camp."

One student poured all his hopes, fears and frustrations into the most beautiful poetry.

The end of the day is also a time for reflection on what the day has brought. Sometimes they think about the bad patches:

"… and then I feel angry with myself."

Others think about their strengths and weaknesses.

"I like to think I'm good at football but I know I'm not."

Others reflect on their happy moments.

"When I've scored the first goal of the day."

and

"When my teacher is pleased and reads my work out because it doesn't happen very often."

Others think about difficulties they may have encountered.

"I don't like change. It throws me off. I get confused and then I get into trouble."

"I don't like falling out with friends and teachers, but I have to stand up for what I think is right."

Lying is frequently used to get out of tricky situations.

"If it's like I'm about to get told off I say I never did it or he started it!"

Parental support

The role parents play in school in the lives of these students is very important and they are happy, in the main, to be supported by them.

"They can find out what is happening and be happy or annoyed."

Support and knowledge can be a two-edged sword, as this student admitted.

"No, I don't like my parents talking to my teachers because they know I've lied and they've let me off."

Arguments with parents mostly centre round instances of poor behaviour, which may well have also alienated friends and family, and make the parents feel they have lost control.

"I try to explain. I didn't mean to do it or that others were doing it more."

"She sends me to my room and I actually didn't do it. I don't like it even if I have done it."

A magic wand

Many of these students would like a magic wand to abolish homework, to make the days shorter and to change *"everything that I'm not good at"*. More specifically, a younger student wants to stop the practice of making them sit on the carpet.

"It's sweaty and there are too many people around me and when I stand up I can't feel my legs."

The main message from these students is that it is important to continue the work of understanding the problems that they have. Most of them are articulate and can often identify what makes life harder for them and why they act as they do. Looking again at teaching and learning styles and trying to fully engage their interest with practical activities and less sitting still listening to the teacher, is a good place to start.

Asperger's syndrome

Asperger's syndrome is described as being at the high-functioning end of autism, thus requiring sensitive handling in the inclusive classroom.

It affects an individual's ability to relate to others, to understand social systems and sometimes to develop normal patterns of speech and language. Asperger's tend to speak in flat tones and have problems using words appropriately in context.

Students with Asperger's syndrome experience difficulties with their social contacts and everyday behaviour. There is a view that it may be more handicapping than autism itself, since individuals have enough language and social understanding to want to be accepted as being the same as everyone else but struggle to make the connections. They can be solitary, eccentric individuals – characterised by their total mismanagement of social interaction – looking past people rather than at them. They often assume that those around them know all about them and what they are thinking. However, they themselves fail to see things from another's point of view.

Their cognitive ability can be average or even high, but their knowledge can be centred in very narrow channels resulting in obsessive interests and ritualistic behaviours.

They also experience heightened sensory awareness and can be intolerant to noise or particular noises as well as over sensitive to textures and light. One student would regularly ask for the strip lights to be switched off, feeling comfortable with low levels of lighting and music of his choice. Others complain that they find black print on white paper disturbing. Many like the labels cut out of their clothing, as they cannot tolerate the feel of them.

There are significantly more boys with Asperger's syndrome than girls (possibly 8 to 1) and their social difficulties tend to make them stand out as unusual. Any change will present major challenges ... but consistent formal approaches will minimise surprises and lead to success.

Students with Asperger's choose to be with others on their own terms. They will quite often shun the company of others, and when they have to participate in group activities such as a class lesson, they may isolate themselves deliberately by turning their back or sitting well away from anyone else.

They find it hard to get 'eye contact' right, either avoiding it at all costs or invading another person's space and staring intently at them.

Some students with Asperger's live in a constant state of anxiety, never quite knowing what to expect or how to deal with situations as they arise. They will often seek or even demand full explanations of routines, timetables and checklists to alleviate the panic that can overtake them. These questions will be repetitive as they gain comfort from hearing the same answer again and again.

Working with current obsessions is often more productive than trying to combat them, but it is important for teachers to acknowledge that it may sometimes be necessary to seek further advice on the management of these pupils. Teachers and parents sometimes benefit considerably from support offered by outreach teams. Their specialist advice can make the difference that will result in students being successfully educated in their current school setting. However, there will always be a small number of students who will need specialist provision and some will benefit most from residential provision with a 24-hour curriculum.

Starting the day

For someone with Asperger's syndrome waking up in holiday time is *"what I dream about!"*. In term time, it is more like a nightmare.

"If it's Tuesday with History, Science and Maths I think oh no, I've got to go to school."

"When I was being picked on I would wake up and think how I would combat it" and *"I want to go back to sleep and avoid contact with other people."*

"When I wake up, I start to worry about what might happen in the day that I haven't planned for. Often I start to scream."

Anxiety permeates nearly all the responses received by this group of students. Thoughts of the day ahead bring little to look forward to, just worry and fear.

" ... frightened – sort of worried something was going to happen. I would expect to get upset at least 3 times a day. I would get upset if someone knocked my desk by mistake ..."

"In mainstream I used to worry about what might happen because I was being bullied."

Getting up in the morning is generally hard, and the organisation of uniform and equipment meets with varying degrees of success.

"I do it, but I'm not very good at it – terrible at it – throw socks down side of bed and spend five minutes trying to find glasses."

"Mum used to do it, now I do most of it."

Equally troublesome can be the texture of materials used in clothing, especially school uniform. They hate clothes that itch or are too hot.

"I didn't like it. It was the mix and match of clothes – my dad's shirt, a tie with staples in it and trousers I'd had since Year 9."

One good thing is that uniform can make them feel less conspicuous and relieve them of the onerous task of choosing fashionable clothes, something they rarely get right.

"I like it. I leave it on when I go home."

Going to school

These students often claim to be bored. Bored because they only want to channel their interests into their current obsession or bored because using this one word, conveniently side steps their difficulties in expressing degrees of feeling.

Setting off for school produced boredom, but also *"I usually dread that something is going to happen which will not be beneficial to me."*

Such a self-centred approach to life is typical. In this world, all that matters is that their needs are met. Even the conversation on the way to lessons has to be directed.

"I usually only talk about one thing – one interest – cars."

The obsessive interests that dominate the lives of these students are very wide-ranging and they can be reluctant to share them once they get to school. They prefer people to observe rather than try to participate. One boy was fascinated by all sorts of keys. He had amassed a huge collection of them and insisted on bringing them to school, all threaded onto a long piece of string. If he was parted from them, he suffered terrible anxiety and was unreachable until he got them back. This was an extreme case, but teachers will be familiar with students who need to have particular things lined up on their desks, or those who are constantly doing something else whilst lessons are in progress. This does not always mean that they have not heard what the teacher is saying. It can mean that it has helped their concentration but it is worth checking as the Asperger's who do suffer from heightened sensory awareness may well find it difficult to do and listen at the same time.

Starting the school day

Most Aspergic students are very reliable about having the correct equipment, mostly, one suspects because they couldn't bear to share with others. They have a tendency to get over anxious and emotional about things which would seem insignificant to other students, like someone moving their bag aside because it is obviously in the way.

On arrival at a new lesson the most important thing is where they are going to sit. They tend to have very strong preferences and dislike any changes to the arrangements. One boy would always choose to sit as close as he could to the teacher for protection, whilst another would always go to the back so that nobody was behind him. Sometimes other individuals cause high levels of stress through no fault of their own.

"I had to sit next to somebody who had cerebral palsy. I felt uneasy because of what he does not have and can't do. I am a perfectionist – I get upset if things aren't perfect. I think I am perfect so I should not sit next to people who aren't."

Perhaps this demonstrates more vividly than any textbook, the rigidity of Aspergic thinking which is, of course, a key characteristic of this specific difficulty.

Because of this focus on self, being required to conform can cause great problems. Tutor/Form time seems to be a particular hotspot. It brings an opportunity to observe others, but also some stress since it is not a lesson and therefore not as structured. Many Asperger students would much rather register briefly and then get on with something else. This poses a dilemma for the form tutor whose job it is to try and integrate them into the group and can take advantage of this time to try and 'programme' their day. However, the Asperger student can value form time because it is not a lesson.

"I finally have time which is not to do with work. I get annoyed when the time is over and I have to work."

Assembly is viewed as annoying and pointless.

Listening to what is being said is difficult sometimes for practical reasons.

"I mostly listen, but because I can't hear certain frequencies I often miss out on what he says."

Similarly, it is this sensitivity to different noise frequencies that can trigger an outburst of temper.

The worst assemblies are remembered for the wrong reasons!

"Worst one was a talk about shoes by Mr ... I think he'd run out of things to do!"

Teachers

Aspergic students like to learn by doing things for themselves, and they have some interesting observations to make about their best and worst teachers. Teachers who are easy to understand are, in fact, the worst since *"they can't keep up with my skill level"*, and do not present a challenge. There are doubts about the competence of some teachers; one student explaining his frustration because the content of the science course at GCSE wasn't detailed enough. He thought this was because the majority of students in the class wouldn't be able to understand, but he could.

Set routines are very important to this group. These are the people who have to know what they can expect next so that they can prepare for it. *"It's a pain if something unexpected happens."* It may take them a long time to accept changes and alterations to the usual routines.

It is also hard for them to accept that what they present in terms of their assignments may often not be wholly relevant to what they have been asked to do. To them, every detail is important, and they can be very resistant to the idea of redrafting coursework that is too long and full of irrelevant detail.

"You work hard at something and people point out the bad things about it."

We sometimes forget just how much effort has been put into a particular task, so praise should always precede criticism. It is not uncommon for a pupil with Asperger's syndrome to rip up an entire page of neat, accurate work because he/she has made an error towards the bottom of the page.

Knowing what is expected in advance is very important; so too are arrangements for handing work in, and woe betide the teacher who makes exceptions to the rules. The best teachers are described as being interesting and making the students do a lot so they are not bored. *"I like the ones who keep order but not by splitting up worst and best pupils. Supply teachers do that …"*

Following a timetable

A timetable can be a safety net, giving a clear structure to the day.

"You know what you have to do next."

It must be explained carefully, otherwise it is seen as yet another thing designed to confuse them.

Some of these students are sticklers for timekeeping and will expect others to be the same, especially their teachers. It's almost as if they cannot cope with time that is unaccounted for. These are the students who arrive early or exactly on time for lessons and are watching the clock at the end so that they can be equally prompt at the next one. They don't mean to be rude … it's just that timekeeping is an important part of their daily ritual. If they are kept behind, or even if they are asked to wait for the bell, this can induce what to others may seem like unreasonable panic.

There may, of course, be a reason for wanting to leave early. Between lessons is a prime time for others to take advantage of their vulnerability.

"It's difficult to arrive at lessons on time because sometimes I've been bullied and I run away – I've been trying to escape."

Others simply don't know how to tell the time.

"Didn't have a watch – only learnt to tell the time in Year 9."

Aspergic students may, as discussed above, find it difficult to conform to an imposed routine – but they all have their own set rituals and routines to which they adhere, which may be difficult for us as 'outsiders' to understand.

"I like doing what I want when I want."

Some never get to grips with the timetable, and this causes them anxiety.

"I never ever have been able to remember the timetable or keep one so I'm always asking what the next lesson is."

I remember clearly one literature lesson when the class was studying the current set book. The previous lesson had been Maths and one Aspergic student was fascinated by the binary system. He continued to work on this, firstly on paper at his desk, and then when this ran out, on the whiteboard in the English classroom. He was totally oblivious to everything else and the teacher, wisely, turned a blind eye to it. The other students did likewise, in an atmosphere of surprising acceptance. The boy reached the conclusion of the problem, returned to his seat and continued with the lesson.

They can all identify their strengths and interests. Many enjoy ICT and are particularly skilled in using computers and other technologies. One student impressed the staff at IBM with his extensive knowledge, whilst others enjoy designing web sites and exploring the Internet.

Reading aloud

Reading aloud is disliked intensely, and provokes a range of feelings. This is often due to the fact that Aspergic students tend to read in a monotone, which meets with ridicule from their peers. One boy persisted in talking and reading in an American accent even though he had never actually lived in the United States.

"I hate it – it makes me nervous." "Makes me worried and queasy."

"People laugh because I read it all the same."

Break-times

Break-times are not enjoyed very much either. Sometimes it is because *"there's nothing to do"* but sometimes it's because this is a time when students can feel vulnerable.

"I go and have a drink and then I hide."

"People laugh at me because I don't know when it's a joke and get upset."

Some spend the time avoiding others.

"If I know someone is hunting me I stay in the toilets but the problem is they don't have locks."

Others need to spend it in exactly the same place, doing or not doing exactly the same activity every day.

Eating with others can be seen as an opportunity to 'connect', to make friends.

"Because you can talk to them and it doesn't get boring or lonely."

"It makes me feel I am needed."

but

"I prefer people to come and sit near me."

However, the talk is often very one sided. The content can be repetitive with the Aspergic student carrying on talking without picking up on the fact that the listener has tuned out. This is another demonstration of friendship on their terms, but occasionally an unusual effort is made.

"I have a conservative taste in food. I like English food, but I learnt to like Chinese food when I had a Chinese friend I taught English to."

This deference to someone else's tastes does not happen often, in fact some students in this category are indifferent to food altogether, regarding meal time as an unwelcome interruption to whatever they are doing and are extremely reluctant to try any new food.

Not all felt tired after lunch. Indeed, one student described how his energy levels rose to the point where he would deliberately do things to seek attention.

"My brain says if you do this you will get in trouble but you want the attention. You pretend you don't like the attention but you do."

Homework

Mostly, they were philosophical about their homework.

"It's to finish off the work you do in the day."

It is a necessary routine and teachers will recognise the student who demands their prep as soon as they enter the classroom. Others hate it.

"I never like it. All it does for me is extend the day."

Some need a distinct break between school and home or living area.

"It is intrusive. It intrudes into my house and I want work to be at school. That's why I feel better when I am boarding."

Homework is also the source of arguments between teachers, parents and their children.

"I don't want to do it!"

"Mum and Dad get angry, especially Dad when he can't do the maths questions."

Confrontation of this kind is unhelpful for most students.

Conversely, when they have completed their homework, they have greater respect for the teacher who has a definite system for taking in and returning their homework and ideally, can be seen to tick their name on a list.

Exams

Examinations are a source of dread for most pupils, but for those with Asperger's syndrome they do provide an expected framework, which can be comforting. The sheer predictability is helpful and they like the peace and quiet and the opportunity to work for a length of time unhindered.

They do however need precise instructions; one boy omitted to turn the page over to complete the exam questions, as there was nothing to tell him he had to.

Social interaction – bullying

Social relationships are a problem, and security at school is dependent on different things for different students.

"I feel safe because I'm older than everyone else."

Friendships do not come easily. Some feel very isolated and try to find a reason for it.

"I never had any friends – people couldn't like me as other people didn't."

Some admit that they irritate others by making inappropriate comments and therefore do not expect to be liked whilst others feel permanently persecuted.

"I start giggling if people get angry. I can't stop and it makes them angrier."

When this happens, the Asperger's student can quickly become a victim – easy prey for some. They often find it difficult to report bullying and assume their parents and school staff already know it is happening and condone it.

Bullies do seem to be particularly drawn to these students, often because they are baffled and unsure how to react to the Asperger's pattern of behaviour. The majority report bullying at some time in their school life and for others it remains a daily problem that they struggle to understand.

"I'll have done something obscure that offends them greatly like kicking a bin or insulting them in some way. I get angry, start swearing. Don't mean to, but I do."

Time to themselves can be a problem, particularly in residential settings where students have a programme of activities following the day's lessons. Some really crave time *"to do their own thing."*

They all admitted to lying. Indeed, this was recognised by one boy as the direct cause of some of his problems.

"People stopped liking me because of my lies."

On some occasions, it appears these lies are actually attempts to say the right things in order to 'fit in'.

It is hard for them to think about and admit to their weaknesses, although some do recognise their problems and some do ask for help.

"How do I get a girlfriend? I'm 17 and I've never had a girlfriend. Tell me what to say."

"I feel pessimistic. I know I've got things wrong."

Teachers can get easily frustrated trying to help these students integrate because as soon as they have taught them an essential skill to cope with a particular set of circumstances, they appear to forget it and are unable to transfer it to a new situation. Hence, they have to be constantly retaught or 'reprogrammed'.

Bedtime

School is exhausting and the universal response to getting home or back to the living area is *"crash in the bed. STOP!"*.

Watching TV and playing computer games offers some relaxation and acts for some as a kind of therapy, although playing computer games can quickly become an obsession and time has to be rationed.

"I can get my light gun out and shoot people and pretend they are people who annoy me. I can do it because it's not real."

They don't need others in the way that most students do, and at the end of the day prefer their own company, or seek others only when they have come to terms with what has happened in the day. Some seek the company of others for a different purpose.

"I try to find people to moan at and try to make them feel guilty about what has happened to me. I talk to the care staff. I rely on them to solve my problems."

Sleep doesn't seem to come easily to them. Although they conform, and go to bed at a reasonable time, many of them reported that it took a long time for them to fall asleep or that they didn't need so much sleep as others.

"It's not easy to sleep ... sometimes I think too much about the next day."

"I always think about the weird process of falling asleep, that I won't wake up or will have a scary dream."

Escaping into a secret world is usually centred on their current obsession which becomes a place of refuge, a place to recover or even a place where they can confront their demons.

"I pretend I am something big, a monster, something huge stepping on people. It makes me feel big and safe and that nobody can hurt me. It's pathetic at fifteen years old."

Parental support

In general they appreciated their parents' involvement in their school life and agreed they were well supported.

"If I had gone to ... I would have become a wreck and needed to go to a mental hospital."

Social communication may not be their strongest point, but their observation and perception of others is interesting in the way it confirms how differently they see the world.

They do, however, shy away from expressing affection physically and if they do it can quickly become inappropriate. One boy who felt particularly comfortable with his Science teacher took to pinging her bra strap as a form of greeting and was reported to his parents. The mother admitted that she had had to tell him it was inappropriate for a boy of his age to kiss her fully on the lips.

A magic wand

Put a magic wand in their hands and two issues emerge above all others. Firstly, the need for a wider range of courses, designed to satisfy their very particular and wide ranging interests/obsessions and needs.

Secondly, the necessity of dealing with bullies in school. One Asperger defined a bully as:

"A person who likes to take out everything on others but never in a nice way."

Which was a perceptive way of expressing what he experienced daily at school.

The last word in this chapter must go to the student who summarised his school life in the following way, simply because I think he speaks for so many.

"It's fun sometimes and at other times absolutely awful."

Dyslexia

Of all the specific learning difficulties, it is probably true to say that more has been written about dyslexia than any of the others. There is a tendency for people to use it as a blanket term to cover a whole range of specific learning difficulties.

Since this condition affects so many, not only those at school, but also adults in all walks of life, the thoughts, views and experiences of dyslexics are important components in any discussion.

In essence, dyslexia can be described as a distinctive pattern of learning difficulties. These are particularly, though not exclusively, associated with the acquisition of reading and spelling strategies. Attainments in these areas are often significantly below what is expected, and great loss of self-esteem ensues as a result.

Under-achievement is probably the single most frustrating element of this condition, affecting both those who try to learn and those who try to teach. It is still not fully understood in some areas of education that teaching dyslexics is a highly specialist skill. Many dyslexics will have a range of difficulties that combine to trip them up in all sorts of ways on all sorts of different occasions. These include difficulties with memory and speech, phonological and language difficulties, difficulties in combining spoken and written language, visual motor problems, short concentration span and social and emotional difficulties. In some cases a family history of learning difficulties exists and must be borne in mind if schools look to parents for support with homework.

It is not difficult to see how this can impact upon students in school where the whole emphasis is on learning and achieving. Add to that the competitive element that exists amongst young people and there is, suddenly, huge potential for disaster for those who cannot make the grade in a society which still emphasises the importance of proving ability through written examinations.

More recently, great strides have been taken to make life more bearable for dyslexic students. Through the tremendous work done by groups like the British Dyslexia Association, The Dyslexia Institute and the countless teachers who commit themselves to specialist teaching, students are more likely to get recognition for their strengths and support for their weaknesses. There is, however, still a lot of work to be done to ensure that all schools are 'dyslexia friendly' and more and more local education authorities are taking this on board.

As the following comments demonstrate, some schools have further to go than others.

Starting the day

On waking, there can be an immediate feeling of panic in term time.

"I must get to school on time."

Thoughts of, *"Is it school? Oh no!"* and *"What do I have to sort out before I go to school?"* can conversely result in overwhelming lethargy.

"If I stay in bed, it will all go away."

On school days, the pressures begin early.

"I'm so comfortable and warm I don't want to get up."

"School is good, but some days are hard because the lessons make me think more."

"I feel stressed and worried."

and

"I feel sad."

Many dyslexics worry about the day ahead and consequently start the day in a negative or anxious frame of mind. Some manage to get themselves organised, but others enlist help.

"I do my uniform, but Mum checks my bag to make sure I have everything."

"I organise myself the night before. I have a timetable on the fridge."

Uniform, although often disliked, can have its benefits.

"I like it. It makes me feel like I belong."

This is important since dyslexic students sometimes feel like outsiders.

"It makes us equal – the same. No-one can bully you because of your clothes."

Going to school

Many students report feeling tired on their way to school. This is often in anticipation of the struggles they expect to encounter during the day, but they do enjoy the thought of being with their friends.

"I'm OK if I'm walking with other people, otherwise I'm anxious."

They mostly chat on their way to school, sometimes about the day ahead, but also *"what I will do after school"*. There are moments of confidence tempered with nagging doubts about what will happen.

"I'm quite often worried. I find lessons difficult and I can't meet coursework deadlines."

*"I'm confident about sport. I worry about work. The writing some-
times worries me and I would rather hang out with my friends."*

"I don't look forward to school."

There was a difference in response here between those in mainstream
schools and those in specialist provision. Those attending specialist schools
catering for dyslexic students report feeling happier with less stress in their
day, as there are so many who can identify with their difficulties.

Starting the school day

Tutor/Form time is the first activity of the day for many students. It is a
time when homework has to be handed in and numerous excuses thought
up. If there is an obvious pattern to these excuses, teachers need to revise
their expectations and differentiate by outcome, gradually extending the
quantity they expect from the dyslexic.

Tutor/Form time is a useful time for dyslexics to use the support to prepare
for the rest of the day.

"I like it. I talk to other people in my group."

"I have to get my diary signed and stuff like that."

"I find it boring. I just think of the weekend or when we go home."

For others, assembly takes place at this time. Some listen to what is said,
but others are miles away.

"I listen if it's important, but sometimes I think about Australia."

*"My mind is thinking about other things like what I'm going to do
with the rest of the day."*

"I think about what I have next and where I have to go and homework."

Others admit to *"going off in my own little world"*. This obviously happens
all through the day, and not just in assembly time.

"I listen, but I also think about other things."

Sometimes, outside speakers can have a big impact.

"A lady came in to tell us about a very bad disease and I wanted to help the people."

Teachers

Teachers can make or break the world of school for the dyslexic pupil. It is not surprising, therefore, that they are very forthright in their comments about their teachers. They prefer teachers who make jokes and keep order within the classroom.

"I like teachers who are kind, but who tell you what you need when you are having trouble concentrating."

They don't like teachers who shout and those that *"make you work on and on for the whole lesson"*.

"I like it when you can talk about anything and they know what you are on about. They're down to earth."

"The teachers who make the lessons fun are the teachers who can joke along and look at it from our point of view and try all sorts of types of games and things and see which works best."

It is well known that the way in which dyslexics are taught is very important. Flexible teachers who are prepared to stray from tried and tested methods and make allowance for the individual's learning strengths, are more likely to experience success and earn the trust and respect of individual students.

"If you have one bad lesson some teachers hold it against you and some give you a fresh start."

Some students genuinely don't remember what happened the previous day or even in the previous hour, so a teacher who is thinking back to some past misdemeanour puzzles them.

The best teachers:

"do things slowly and come and explain again if you don't understand."

They are

"kind and easy to understand."

The worst teachers are:

"strict and won't let you go to the toilet. They're not easy to understand."

"They talk for ages and that's bad because I switch off."

"I like listening and doing. I find it difficult to read and follow instructions."

"I think I learn more by listening because I find writing so hard."

"I like it when somebody talks to me separately."

This last comment is particularly pertinent because a lot of dyslexics find it hard to relate to instructions given to the whole class. Often, if a teacher gives more than one instruction at a time, they get hopelessly lost in the sequence and simply repeating the list of instructions doesn't help. They need to break down and understand each one.

Writing oral instructions down in clearly structured steps or making a diagrammatic cue card can help understanding and act as a memory trigger to keep dyslexic students on track. Using different coloured pens on a whiteboard for each line of writing is another helpful strategy. You do have to check that the colours used can be seen from all parts of the room and not demand excessive copying from the board.

"When I look at work I have had to copy from the board, I can't understand what I have written. There are so many mistakes."

Following a timetable

Asked if they liked following a timetable, they all said yes because it helps them to know in advance what they are going to have to do and where they need to go. This is very important for dyslexics, because many of them have little concept of time.

"If you don't know what lesson to go to you could go to the wrong one and I worry about that."

"The timetable makes me feel organised."

"I don't like following it all the time – but it would be a lot more complicated without one."

A significant number find it difficult to arrive at lessons on time. Some dawdle and forget where they are going. It helps them to have a time lapse between lessons (some schools have a five-minute change over time). It is unhelpful when teachers keep students late so that they are separated from the group.

This is because some are totally reliant upon others to guide them to where they need to be.

"It's hard to arrive on time because there are lots of people in the way."

Changing rooms from one lesson to another provides an opportunity for a change of scene which most students like. The main problem is that the right equipment has to move with them.

"I'm all right. My mum makes sure I have the right stuff."

"I try to make sure I have all the equipment so I am ready."

On arrival at the new lesson, it takes some time for students to settle down, to adjust to a change of subject and teacher and to find the equipment they need.

"It takes me a long time to settle down. It takes time to find my stuff."

"In English and Maths it takes me time to settle down."

In some lessons the students are directed to where they should sit; in others they have a choice.

"I don't like sitting next to people who copy your work."

"I like sitting in the place where I always sit. It matters who I sit next to because some people are silly and then the teacher will think I am silly and I will get into trouble."

Some select certain places because

"I need a lot of help so I sit near the front."

"I have to be near the window."

"I prefer to sit in the middle row so I don't always get asked questions."

Reading aloud

Some students hate doing this, but others will tolerate it. It seems to depend on the atmosphere that is created in the classroom. Dyslexic students feel very exposed when asked to read in front of others, so they will only do it willingly if they feel that those around them understand that they have a problem and will offer help and support as soon as it is needed.

"I hate it. I'm not good at reading. I panic, especially if I have to do it in front of my friends. I'm really slow."

"I hate reading aloud but I go head to head and battle my fear."

"I hate reading aloud. I get nervous and worry. I end up reading words that aren't on the page."

Students in specialist provision clearly find it easier.

"I didn't used to like it before I came to a school where everyone finds it difficult."

For most, however, it is simply a nightmare.

"I'd ask first do I have to do it? It makes me feel anxious and I know that it will be too hard."

"I can read a word on one page and then forget what it is when I see it again so people laugh."

Keeping track of text is a major problem and keeping up with everyone else causes major anxiety. All the students we spoke to reported a level of nervousness, but some are braver than others.

"I feel nervous – but I don't make a big fuss about it."

Perhaps it is time to consider the validity of making students read aloud. As adults we rarely do it. The skill is in reading successfully – silently. This is the skill we wish to encourage, but some students never get there because they have been scared off. As teachers, we need to create a helpful, forgiving atmosphere in the classroom; one where we can invite students to read aloud and if they don't want to, to be able to pass to somebody who does.

Break-times

For some students this is a surprisingly busy time. It is a time to eat, a time to collect things for the next lesson and a time (in theory) to use the toilet. In practice, many dyslexics will genuinely forget, run out of time and either arrive late at the next lesson or irritate the teacher with requests to go to the toilet immediately the lesson begins.

It can be a time to see a teacher *"because I don't understand something"*. However, teachers need to acknowledge that dyslexic pupils tire easily due to the greater demands on them and need their breaks and it is better to arrange a separate time to put in the individual help although this can be difficult logistically.

Break-time is also a time to meet with friends again.

"I love them. It's a time to chill out, talk to your friends and play around."

For some, fifteen minutes just isn't long enough.

"I'd like to have 25 minutes for break instead of 15."

However, others can run into problems when they act impulsively and fail to anticipate the outcome of their actions.

Lunchtime is seen as an important social time, giving opportunity to speak to both their friends and their teachers. Talking to teachers for some is

"not so great because you have to be polite and stuff".

Some, however, recognise the value of talking to others.

"It's good to talk to somebody at the table; it's good to socialise."

A few students do not see it this way, commenting on the difficulties they have.

"I don't have enough time to eat and there are too many people queuing up."

"I don't like eating in front of other people."

Interestingly, quite a large number of students say they feel tired after lunch. They think that the day is too long *"especially if it's hot"* and some are already beginning to lose track of where they are in the day.

"Have we had lunch?"

Homework

Some dyslexics are philosophical about homework, accepting that it has to be done so *"you'll learn more"*, but for others it is something that they dread.

"Homework is a pain. There are other things I want to do."

Some find it extraordinarily difficult to work independently and prefer to do it at school where there is help available. Others are so tired at the end of the day that it becomes a chore.

"I never really feel like it as I have been working hard all day."

"I hate getting a lot of homework. If I write it down, I can't make out what I have written and if they write it down, I don't always understand what to do."

"I never have the right books and everyone gets cross with me."

Some subjects are more accessible than others; for example Art is cited several times as being the most enjoyable subject to do for homework.

Dyslexics welcome alternative means of recording their ideas. Working on laptops or even tape recorders helps, but still for some homework is the least enjoyable part of the day, causing difficulties and arguments with teachers and parents.

"My parents get on my case if I don't do it and I tell them to get off my back."

Spelling difficulties can really put them off attempting to put their thoughts on paper and attempting to use a wider and more imaginative vocabulary. Words that have been recently learnt for tests are quickly forgotten in the process of being creative.

It seems that *"getting down to it"* is the biggest problem of all.

They want to choose when to do it, and that isn't always possible. They also experience considerable problems with estimating how long it will take and therefore run out of time.

"Everything takes so long."

Many would identify with this final comment.

"Sometimes I get it for not doing it!"

Exams

Examinations are an important part of every student's life, but dyslexics feel very strongly that their results give a false picture of their capabilities. Their response to exams ranges from *"they're all right"* to *"absolutely terrified"*.

Linking back to the problems they experience with homework, it is the lack of support and immediate help that throws them. It is like jumping without a parachute. Indeed, this is a good analogy since so much depends on final grades at GCSE. With all the media hype, it is hard to convince students that getting anything less than a 'C' is worthwhile, even though a lower grade may be a considerable achievement in the face of their individual difficulties.

Remembering what they have learnt is the major problem and being confident that they can retrieve it from their long-term memory.

*"I might forget what's been said and everything will leave my head
and I'll get zero."*

Many students have real problems keeping track of the examination timetables and for some, the whole thing is simply a nightmare.

"I am terrified. I go all shaky and get really angry with myself."

This is a common and very telling response. Knowing that they are likely to let themselves and everybody else down produces a sickening fear and loss of confidence. It is no wonder that so many describe themselves as scared, wary, terrified and nervous. All these are emotions which make accessing rational thought and long-term memory hard, if not impossible.

Not one dyslexic student that I know or spoke to in the course of writing this book, feels easy with exams. Most report high levels of stress and the sinking feeling that they will let themselves down. They need to be prepared from an early age. Teaching relaxation techniques and other practical strategies for getting through this stressful time are an essential part of the revision process. Familiarity with past papers and understanding the language used are vital for dyslexic students. They need to experience these within the safe confines of their classrooms before they are exposed to them in the examination room.

A number of dyslexic students are entitled to concessions. They really need them and often value highly the opportunity to demonstrate their ability.

"Exams are OK as long as I can read them and understand what to do. An LSA read last week. That really helped."

"I can't do this without somebody to read and write for me."

Social interaction

In general, most dyslexic students interact well with others. Many of them exude a social confidence that belies their literacy difficulties. The speaking and listening elements of English GCSE hold no terrors for some. If they can speak, they can share some of their deepest thoughts and ideas.

For others, however, it is not so easy. Although reluctant to admit they have actually been bullied, some admit to being victims of name-calling and rudeness, which is usually sorted out by their teachers. Some have experienced problems in the past.

"It used to happen to me, but it has stopped now I have moved school."

"It used to happen to me. Sometimes it still does, but I get on with it now."

There is a feeling that it happens and it isn't fair.

"It's not fair to bully people."

"There is name-calling but it doesn't happen to me. The older boys take it as a joke but the younger boys don't."

Social skills are viewed as strengths by most of them.

"I've got lots of friends."

"I help people if they're in a tough situation."

They are aware of their weaknesses too. Reading, writing, spelling and English are top of the list!

"I'm not very organised. I'm not really good at football."

"I take everything too seriously. I'm annoying."

Their happiest moments are naturally when they succeed, particularly if they have to overcome significant difficulties to do it.

In general, a routine is expected and enjoyed, but a significant number admit to liking the excitement of something different happening.

"Unexpected things are good. We get lots of warning if that is going to happen."

One or two are thrown by changes in routine.

"I feel annoyed if I have to do something completely different from what I've been doing."

The most difficult times are when they have to confront difficulties.

"When I'm not sure what to do."

"When I forget my work to hand in"

and

"When it gets too boring and I get fed up."

In company with others they lie to get themselves out of sticky situations.

"Everybody does, don't they?"

"I do tell lies, but not bad lies."

Friends are regarded as the most important part of their support network.

"They support me and I support them."

"We're all the same, all dyslexic and stuff, no pressure."

Acceptance of one another's problems and difficulties is seen as a prime reason for friendship as is the encouragement that they offer one another.

"They encourage me to do the things I want to do."

Bedtime

At the end of the day, they are all really tired, describing themselves as *"relieved"* and *"totally finished!"*, most of these students need to change out of uniform, eat a meal and watch TV. Some need to be on their own or with their pets. *"I like to see my dog."* Pets can have a therapeutic effect making different demands on them, none of which involve the written word. Some need to be with people.

"It wouldn't be good if you weren't with somebody to talk to."

Most are so tired at the end of the day that they don't have much trouble settling down to sleep. However, there are those worriers who do find it hard to sleep, thinking about the next day and *"sometimes I think about my worst subjects"*.

Others escape into a secret world.

"It is a world of battles and lots of things happening."

"My secret world is a road with leaves falling. It is a nice place."

"I escape into my video collection of "Only Fools and Horses."

"I make up stories in my head."

Parental support

Parental support is important. *"If I have problems they tackle them."*

Their involvement in school matters can be good or bad.

"She's embarrassing, saying she's proud of me to the teachers."

"They tell me that I can be what I want. No limits!"

"They're helping me with my reading, to go to a better college, to get a better job and to be more successful."

Tension can build up if a parent does not fully accept the strain being dyslexic can put on their child and has unrealistic expectations of what they can achieve.

"Mum says work harder, and I'm saying I'm working as hard as I can."

A magic wand

What student wouldn't want a magic wand to change things to their liking? Top of the dyslexic list of changes is no homework, and less time at school. Others are more specific.

"I want everybody to be really kind to me. If I had three wishes, I would want no homework, kind teachers and more playtimes!"

"I want a bigger football pitch."

"More exciting lessons."

Finally, two students made comments that I feel sum things up really well. The first was in specialist provision:

"I'm glad I'm here and not at a big school in a class with teachers who don't understand and who call me 'special needs boy' like they did at my old school."

The second was in a dyslexia-friendly Comprehensive:

"They try not to expect a lot, but they do expect the best efforts."

Dyspraxia

Recognition of dyspraxia comes when students have poor coordination and balance without any obvious physical or perceptual causes. They tend to appear untidy and somewhat ungainly around the school, which may focus unwelcome attention on them. Most tasks take longer for them to process and carry out.

They experience significant problems with self-organisation, especially with regard to keeping their possessions together, and in an acceptable state. Their school bags can be chaotic, bulging with unmarked, dog-eared homework that they have either forgotten to do or to hand in. They have often taken longer to decide which hand to write with and coupled with their poor fine motor coordination, their handwriting can be slow or illegible (or both!).

They have significant problems with setting work out on a page.

"Literacy Hour was made just to torment me. I have felt like killing myself. I get so angry. They all think I am stupid but I am not."

Ultimately, many dyspraxic students find that a word processor helps with the presentation of written work and some may seek the concession of using one to produce coursework as well as for their examination scripts.

Spatial tasks such as map work, measuring and estimating may present difficulties. In some lessons, such as Science and Design Technology, where standards of safety and precision are required, their clumsiness is likely to be an issue of great concern and specialist advice may be required.

Often, the area in which they experience the most difficulty is PE, especially those lessons that involve team games. Self-esteem can sink to an all-time low, as they tend to be picked last for teams. This is due to others being all too aware of their poor coordination, and the fear that their contribution to the team effort will be minimal. Further disruption can ensue when they arrive late for the next lesson as changing can be a nightmare, getting clothes inside out or a sweater the wrong way round, managing buttons, shoelaces and other fastenings present a real challenge.

They inevitably look untidy and appear clumsy, looking awkward when they run.

In school, dyspraxia marks the individual out as being unable to do lots of the normal age appropriate activities such as riding a bicycle, catching a ball, competitive sports and playing a musical instrument. Such students will soon come to the notice of their peers and teachers and may well be criticised by those, who lack awareness of the condition, for being inept and careless.

Starting the day

Waking up in holiday time presents no problems – just happy anticipation of enjoyable activities and thinking, *"this is the best time of my life because I can do whatever I want"*. In term time, though, it is a different story.

"Sometimes I thought that I couldn't take school any more, and wished I could skip it."

Thinking of the day ahead raises anxieties, with students expressing their worries in such terms as *"worried about PE"*, *"head feels heavy"* and commenting:

"I would often wonder if I could make it through the day and then count the days after, until the weekend."

Like most of their peers, they all find it hard to get up in the morning. However, feats of organisation confront them, beginning with organising their uniform. Some have a system of doing it the night before – but others rely on help from others.

"Mum does it. If she is going away my gran does it."

None feel comfortable in their uniform. It is recognised that dyspraxics often experience heightened sensory awareness. This can apply particularly to the texture of some materials, labels rubbing the neck and cuffs irritating the wrist.

"I feel trapped in my uniform."

"I worry about the tie and the shoes – I can't tie the laces."

The tie and the shoes seem to present the greatest difficulties, but there can be other worries.

"I always get my blazer dirty."

Resigned to such problems, they acknowledge the difficulties they have in keeping clean and tidy.

Going to school

On the way to school some feel happy, others are tired, but others feel nothing but dread:

"The fact that I knew I would have to deal with so many people who were hostile towards me."

Some make a point of not thinking about school at all …

"I tell myself it's not important."

Others will only confide in one or two particular friends who they can trust.

"I wouldn't talk to many people in the first three years. In the last two years I made a good friend who I could talk to."

Because of their difficulties, it is not unusual for them to take longer to establish friendships as peers tend to be wary of their slow reactions.

Starting the school day

It is a relief to arrive, hopefully with the right equipment at lessons, their tutor bases or form rooms. Some are pleased to be with their friends, whilst others rely more on their teachers, realising that adults may be more sympathetic to their difficulties.

"… my tutor was a good guy and didn't mind me hanging around in his class."

Most admit to worrying when thinking about the day ahead, but try to instil in themselves a feeling of confidence.

"I do worry but I try to feel confident with my friends around me."

In assembly, they like to listen to the stories that have a moral. They dislike it when assembly is used for complaints and telling people off and one student *"... thought it was pointless ... ."* One of the difficulties here is that often students are very uncomfortable in assembly halls. Sitting cross-legged, or on benches without fidgeting can present a real challenge and be almost impossible for dyspraxics.

Teachers

The teacher's personality is of paramount importance, particularly their form teacher to whom they feel they should be able to look for help and support.

"I like my teacher. I don't like substitute teachers."

" ... the teacher is always shouting at us. I'm thinking 'God help me, she's shouting at us again!' "

"I had a stricter form teacher that was difficult to approach. I don't think I ever talked to her."

Going from class to class they observe how different teachers conduct their lessons and manage their classrooms.

"They sat me with my back to the class and the board for a long time and my mum had to tell them."

"I prefer teachers who teach rather than made you colour in or just make you write it down from the board."

The students are very clear, and often perceptive about what makes a good or a bad teacher.

"My favourite teachers are the teachers who don't mind you asking them questions."

"I like teachers in the lessons I can do."

"The worst teachers are the ones who never listen to opinion and only dictate."

"Some teachers don't explain well. It's as if they think we are 18."

"I like teachers who don't nag and who don't keep me in and who say things clearly and wait. I don't like teachers who rush and set too hard work."

Students with dyspraxia need more time to understand what they have to do, to process oral instructions. Sometimes they have to check that they have the correct information and often they will need more time to do the task that is set. It is very easy to overlook these basic needs when teachers are rushing to meet the next deadline.

Following a timetable

The timetable is generally regarded as helpful, particularly for the first few weeks of a term or a year, but for some, though it should be the key to improving their organisation, it is of little or no help whatsoever. They find it hard to access the information which involves reading both vertically and horizontally.

"I never know when swimming is or if it is non-uniform day. My mum writes it on the calendar but even then we get it wrong."

Dyspraxics often have a poor awareness of time and this, coupled with the fact that their poor spatial awareness makes a timetable hard to follow, results in comments such as:

"I just go when the bells go!"

Changing rooms for lessons does not seem to be a problem in itself, as they can follow the herd, but dyspraxics find it difficult to arrive with the correct equipment.

"I know I won't have the right things or the right homework."

"I forget my pen frequently."

"If I didn't have the right equipment I would borrow it from some-one."

Settling down in lessons is not seen as a significant issue for most, but all have strong opinions on whom they like to sit with. Whilst the majority insisted on sitting with their friends, others want to be on their own.

"I would prefer to sit at the rear of the class on my own. I would pre-fer to sit on my own."

This may well result from a reluctance to let a peer witness their ineptitude at a task which others find easy, e.g. using scissors or copying from the board.

Reading aloud

Reading aloud is almost universally disliked. It makes students feel *"nerv-ous"*, *"uncomfortable"* and *"bad"*. Some mention feeling embarrassed *"and I feel people will laugh at me. I often have a dry throat"*.

"My statement says they shouldn't make me do this. I can't do it any-way."

Many dyspraxics will have trouble reading. Common problem areas are losing their place and struggling to read with expression. Small wonder that it is so unpopular.

Break-times

Often, these are far from *'a break'*, depending on the dyspraxic's level of self-confidence and whether they feel accepted by their peers or suspect that they are seen as something of an oddity. Break-times are *"OK when no-one bullies me"*. There should be an option to stay in away from the crowd.

"I hated large groups of people." "I'm always falling over." " They go mad when I bump into them." "Sometimes, I can't say what I mean – it comes out wrong."

Some, again, feel safer close to adults and clearly do not enjoy rushing around like the others. Lunchtime also causes some tensions.

"The food comes on a plate with all the things on and I don't like it because it's not the way I have it so I take sandwiches."

Not liking the food can be related to their sensitivity to texture:

"Lumps or slimy foods, urgh!"

It can also be a time when they are sensitive to teasing due to their poor co-ordination, which can result in anti-social table manners, eating with fingers and failing to shut their mouth.

"I don't have any of my own so I'm not sure what good table manners are."

Some like to eat with their close friends, whilst others hate being with their peers or can only tolerate it under certain conditions *"...only if there's no talking"*. After lunch, some are tired. Everything takes more effort, moving around the school, keeping their possessions safe, and making the appropriate responses so some are more candid:

"No, not tired, just fed up!"

Homework

Homework is disliked intensely. Most of the dyspraxic students I interviewed couldn't see the point of it. In this, they were in line with most of their peers. Comments varied from *"I have done enough work during the day"* to *"some homeworks are more pointless than others"*.

Generally, homework caused problems between the students and the teachers who set it.

"They sometimes shout at me because I do not manage to finish it in time."

"I thought I had given it in, I don't know where it is."

"It gets crumpled in my bag and then teachers get cross."

Exams

To some, the set organisation of exams appeals. They have a clear structure and specific instructions. It is the revision that throws them and the somewhat daunting formal atmosphere.

"I don't like silence and I don't like the teachers breathing down my neck when they walk around the classroom."

Others are acutely aware of their dependence on the support they get.

"I get extra time and support, but I would worry without that."

Social interaction – bullying

Initially, it may well be hard for dyspraxics to 'fit in' for reasons already stated in this chapter. It takes longer for them to settle in and be accepted by their peers.

All reported instances of bullying.

"It happens to me, I don't know who else. An invitation to a party was on the floor and I couldn't find it as it was on the floor and two girls were laughing at me."

"I don't like it … recently I've found ways to confront them."

"There's always bullies – happens to everyone."

"I try to ignore them."

After school, the strain of 'fitting in' all day causes some to just crave time on their own.

"I would spend some time in my room listening to music."

At the end of the day they are glad it is over. Some feel relief, others are fed-up whilst some just look forward to going to bed. By and large they are able to confide in friends or parents.

"I used to talk to my Nan about how much my headmaster wanted to expel me" but not *"the care staff as they never do anything about it".*

Bedtime

Going to bed at the prescribed time is not a problem, but sleep does not come easily.

"I go to bed at 9.30 and go to sleep at midnight."

"My mum tells me to relax and wind down but I have bad dreams and I am scared to sleep."

A secret world into which they can escape often provides some relief.

"I am always somewhere else. I have so many schemes and plans."

"My martial arts was always my world that no-one knew about."

Self-confidence and self-esteem are important for everyone, and feelings at the end of the day depend on what sort of day we have had.

"I got through the day and survived."

"Happy to be home … angry about school, sometimes upset."

"If things go well I feel happy and if they don't I feel really annoyed."

All the dyspraxics interviewed could name their strengths.

"Coping with stuff and keeping my cool."

"Creative – I write good stories and I paint."

"Playing on the computer" and *"I'm a good friend to people".*

Asked to identify what they thought their weaknesses were, some replied as others would, by naming their worst subjects, but others took the opportunity to be more precise and personal. One said he was no good at *"learning in lessons and fighting – can't fight properly"*. Another went right to the heart of this disability and said he couldn't do *"two-handed tasks"*.

But there are clearly happier moments. One mentioned *"sleep time as I'm very tired at the end of the day, also lunch!"*. Others said being with friends was the best bit, whilst another singled out giving a power-point presentation in assembly.

Contrary to what some people think, these students quite like their routines being disrupted. Clearly, they are not dependent on routines dominating their day.

"I'm OK if the photographer comes as lessons stop and that is good – unless it's creative writing – but I don't like new teachers."

There are other positive aspects as well.

"If something different happens it makes it a tiny bit more interesting!"

Worst moments included least enjoyed lessons, homework and

"teasing, bullying, getting things wrong – everybody hates me".

Not surprisingly, games and PE were cited as the least favourite subjects.

They were asked if they ever lied to get themselves out of tricky situations. All admitted to doing this sometimes. They clearly felt a degree of shame to some extent, but saw it as a survival strategy. Friends were declared to be very important and part of a mutual support network.

"They never try and pressure me."

"It's got better since I made a friend – they are very important."

"Friends are very important to me as it is the first school I've really had any proper friends."

All this prompts the question, do we, as adults, sometimes underestimate the importance of this and focus our attention on academic issues? We cannot make friends for our children, but it is important to be aware of a child's isolation and support them in other ways.

Parental support

Parents in the main, were seen as part of the support network.

"… if they weren't (involved) I wouldn't be here."

"My mum goes up to the school and it gets better for a time."

Some prefer their parents not to be too involved, although they like them to be *"always at the end of the phone if I want them"*.

Disagreements with parents are part of the teenage territory, but there is an inevitability about what causes the disagreements for dyspraxics.

"We argue about me losing items and why I don't do my homework better."

"I've lost three PE kits this term."

"I have a new pen almost every day."

"I want them to educate me at home, but they make me go to school and do PE. You can have lessons at home."

A magic wand

"If I had a magic wand I would get rid of … uniform, homework, the headmaster!"

Not one used their magic wand in a positive way to provide them with things they wanted. It seems that their world is just full of unwanted pressures, making life difficult for the majority of the time.

Speech and language difficulties

A speech and language difficulty is a term that can describe a range of problems. These are all to do with acquiring language and developing the ability to communicate. In turn, this affects a student's ability to access education.

Language disorders affect communication in a wide variety of ways, and those who have problems in organising and understanding language may find that the difficulties persist into adulthood.

Word finding difficulties occur when people have problems retrieving words from their memory when they need them in order to communicate accurately.

Pragmatics is the area of language that focuses on how people communicate in real situations in an appropriate manner.

All language-impaired students are likely to have some pragmatic difficulties, but some need specific help with things such as initiating conversations, using the appropriate forms of address and turn taking. Others have difficulties keeping conversations on track and may not recognise the intent of others, for example in greeting, teasing or questioning.

The educational implications are vast, since everyone needs to develop a language for learning. Some students will need specialist help with teachers using simple language structures that gradually lead to tasks that demand greater complexity. Supporting language development needs to be on a broad base since every aspect of the day is involved.

Replies to our questions often appear brief as many students lacked the language skills to elaborate.

Starting the day

Those with speech and language problems wake in term time with their thoughts dominated by the day ahead and how they will cope with it. *"I'm still tired. Lessons ... yuk!"*

"I don't like Mondays because I know I have the whole five days ahead of me."

"I don't like Tuesday because of Science and English."

It is sometimes hard for them to get up, and organising their uniform and equipment sometimes poses problems.

"Mum does it at home, I don't do it at school!"

"I do it with a bit of help."

The uniform is tolerated by most, but not by all!

"It's horrible! I wish they'd get rid of the tie."

"My uniform is all crinkly."

"The jacket feels different to the jumper. It's more grown up."

Going to school

It is on the way to school that tiredness seems to set in, accompanied by nervousness and a sense of resignation at the day ahead.

"I'm back at this place again like millions of times before."

Many of these students spend their day confused and bewildered because they get the wrong end of the stick and misunderstand what is said to them. Quite often they miss instructions that are given to the class because they don't realise that they are directed at them. It is because of this that they often start the day in a bit of a fog and do not particularly look forward to what is ahead. They feel resigned to whatever is in store for them.

"I just get on with it."

Starting the school day

For most of these students, the day begins with Tutor/Form time when the main task is to *"figure out what lessons I have that day"*. The problem for some of them is that if they are confused about something, they do not always have the words to ask their tutor or friends for help. They tend to stay on the edge of the group, reluctant to join in with group discussions or to share experiences.

"I don't want to talk to the others in my group. I get lost in the middle of what I'm saying and it's embarrassing."

"I know what I mean, but I get in a muddle and it comes out all wrong."

They are happier listening to others than joining in, because they often lack the words to say exactly what they mean, and in the end they give up altogether, often saying, *"it doesn't matter"*. Noise can further exacerbate their problems with communication.

Assembly isn't always that riveting, especially if the language used is hard to understand.

"Sometimes I listen, but sometimes it blurs out of place so I think about what I'm going to do at the weekend."

This is an important issue. If these students are to learn and understand and benefit from what is presented to them, the language used needs to be appropriate. This does not necessarily mean that it should be simple, but articulation must be clear and concepts explained again if necessary. It is easy to assume that students have understood, when they really haven't. They develop a way of getting by through imitating their peers. Although at times when they are tired and their coping strategies are exhausted, they can appear to be 'out of it' and in a world of their own.

Checking out the precise meaning of words and phrases can be done within the group without drawing attention to individuals. It is good practice to invite someone to explain the meaning of a word, and then if they can't, to supply the meaning yourself. However, if you have serious concerns, it is vital that they are assessed and receive appropriate help from a speech and language therapist so that vital learning time is not lost and they fall further behind their peers.

Teachers

Teachers sometimes forget to think about the language they use when teaching. These students are aware of what helps them to learn.

"I like pictures and doing things and just a bit of talking."

"I like to see someone else doing it."

"The worst teachers talk on and on and then they start all over again and you still don't understand."

For students who have a poor grasp of language, just listening is very diffi-cult and it is unlikely that they will remember what they have heard. Many of them like to picture what they are learning so that they don't have to rely on words alone.

"I listen a bit, I don't like writing, but I do like pictures."

It may come as a surprise to learn that many of these students like to experiment with the language they do have.

"I love writing stories and making them exciting."

Sometimes they will use the wrong word, but sensitive teachers *"help me to choose better words and tell me how to spell them."*

The best teachers *"know loads of history"* and *"are funny".*

"They give you time to answer and help you when you forget a word so your friends don't see."

"When they get cross they don't suddenly yell at you!"

"The worst teacher is grumpy and shouty."

"The best teachers are easy to understand. The worst ones are not easy to understand."

"I would like to be taught by having fun as well!"

Teachers have a huge responsibility to connect with all the students in their care, and to make sure that they are communicating effectively, particularly with those whose own language skills are impaired. Sometimes, pupils with speech and language difficulties can unintentionally appear rude as their language lacks the social niceties. At other times, they become genuinely upset when they cannot find the words they want to express themselves clearly. They want to be supported in a sensitive way without being patronised.

Following a timetable

Most of these students agree that the timetable is of great help. Following it is a necessity because *"if I didn't I'd go and play football all day!".*

"I like following a timetable because it helps to organise me!"

Arriving at lessons on time is quite a problem, as many of these pupils have little or no concept of time. They need visual reminders of how the day is broken up and frequent prompts as to what point they have reached in it. Words like 'yesterday', 'tomorrow', 'before' and 'after' confuse them. Many of them rely on their friends to remind them when and where to go. Sometimes the school organisation itself makes this more difficult than it should be.

"It is difficult to arrive on time because in English we have three different rooms to go to."

For those with any sort of learning difficulty, arrangements like this are very hard to cope with.

Room changes result in the inevitable organisational problems with school bags, pens and pencils easily being mislaid.

"I don't always have the right stuff, but I'm not worried about it. I just borrow from others."

Arriving at a new lesson means that students have to find somewhere to sit.

"I like sitting at the front so that I can listen."

"I don't like sitting next to annoying people, ones who poke you."

"I like to sit next to Matthew because he tells me what to do so I can understand."

"I like to dig in straight away. I really don't mind where I sit."

Any changes to the timetable can cause problems because of the reliance that some students place on it. It takes some of them a long time to understand where they should be, and changes can throw them completely. They need plenty of warning and clear explanations of exactly what will happen that is different.

Each individual has different requirements and teachers should not underestimate the value of peer mentoring.

Reading aloud

These students hate reading aloud.

"I hate it. I don't want to talk in front of people. I don't feel nervous, I just feel as if I'll do something wrong. I can't even read what I've written."

"I don't like reading aloud because I get all worried."

"It sounds odd."

Speaking and listening activities as well as reading aloud hold particular terrors for this group of students. For many of them it is their worst nightmare because they struggle so much with language. Some have quite good reading skills, but because their comprehension of what they read is impaired, they feel vulnerable in front of their peers.

Break-times

Break-time is a welcome relief for some students.

"Great, it's break and I can do whatever I want!"

"The break-times are all right because you don't have to work for fif-teen minutes."

For others, however, it is neither a relief nor a pleasure. They don't necessarily have much to do, and they don't have the skills to socialise easily with their peers. A joke or complicated game leaves them feeling left out as they cannot unravel the language or sequence of events and respond appropriately. In addition, they find it hard to tell someone else a story about something that has happened to them. They tend to muddle the verb tenses and often assume the listener knows more than they do, leaving out information vital to the understanding of what they are trying to say.

"I don't like break-times."

"I go to the fish pond."

Sadly, for some it is a time of heightened isolation when they seek only their own company.

"I go to the library."

"I like to be on my own. I think about my next lesson and I can be there first."

Unfortunately, some resort to physical aggression when they cannot find the words to resolve a situation.

Homework

Homework is unanimously disliked.

"There is not much point of homework from my point of view. There probably is from the teacher's point of view but it just makes more work for them so they probably hate it too."

Nobody enjoys homework.

"Why would you enjoy it?"

"I do homework as soon as I get it. I don't see the point of it because we work all day then have extra pressure."

"I just have to do it."

"It gets in the way of my time at home."

"I do not like any homework. Most of the time, I refuse to do it."

" I find it hard to find out what to do and then I can't think of the words."

One is tempted to think that the homework that is set does not achieve a great deal in terms of learning. Indeed, some parents have also made it clear that they think homework should not be set because of the enormous tensions it creates within the family, particularly at weekends.

Exams

Examinations cause a lot of pressure and tension. There is an issue here about the wording of some questions, since they seem to be designed to confuse with complex sentences, embedded clauses and passive constructions. Pupils with speech and language difficulties instantly lose confidence in their ability to know anything. Many of these students have a fragile hold upon language. In a tense situation, they are unable to cope with badly structured questions that use complex vocabulary. It is not surprising, therefore, that exams are described as *"horrible"* and *"annoying"*.

"I get really nervous and find it really hard to revise."

"I hate them. I get worried and upset."

"I hate them because I feel under pressure."

"I don't feel so good."

There are few who feel positive about exams and tests. Some admit to thinking *"they're OK"*, whilst taking the philosophical view that *"we have to do them, don't we?"*.

Social interaction

For those with speech and language problems, normal everyday social interaction is not the automatic process that it is for others. Although some seek the company of others, many keep their distance and really need time on their own.

They do not always know how to use common courtesies, and will operate in social situations on their own terms.

"At lunch-time I like to eat my food as fast as I can so that I can get out to break."

Some do become victims and suffer name-calling and other forms of bullying.

"People tease me and I get upset."

"People say offensive stuff to me."

"Some people call me NAZA or Greenpeace."

They can be oblivious to the more sophisticated insult but all too often become hypersensitive.

"It happens to me, I don't know who else ... two girls were laughing at me."

Some manage to survive by developing coping strategies and can look back and remember.

"It used to happen to me, but now it's stopped."

Students who have these difficulties can only look on as others conduct their relationships with apparent ease. For some it is not that much of a problem, but for others it is a constant source of worry and bewilderment and some will spend their whole lives wondering why it was all so difficult.

Friends are important as they ensure that there is always a network of support in place.

"My friends are kind."

"All my friends support me."

"They support me. They don't put pressure on me."

But not everybody can count on this sort of support, especially if making friends is a problem.

"My friends hardly ever support me. I don't see them a lot."

"It is sometimes not a nice community because other pupils pick on me because they think I'm a 'boff' because I ask lots of questions."

"I'm not happy with my friends as they don't play with me."

These responses indicate that there are probably more students who feel isolated at school than we realise. Some of them are very good at covering up their unhappiness. They are very reluctant to admit to this problem and will only do so when encouraged by somebody they really trust.

Speech and language therapists and one to one teachers are a vital resource for these students, helping them to understand and come to terms with their difficulties and to develop coping strategies.

Bedtime

At the end of the day, these students tend to be extremely tired because of the extra effort they have had to put in to follow what has been said to them during the long day. They need the opportunity to relax.

"I have hot chocolate and lie on my sofa."

"I play on my computer or watch TV."

The day's activities are sometimes discussed with friends or parents, but not always. They have had enough of *'talking'*.

"I don't talk to anyone ... too tired!"

"After school I try to forget about it completely."

"I want to keep school there and home here."

"I go to bed at ten o'clock and I cannot get to sleep that easy. I do not think about school the next day."

"I go to bed at 9.30 when I am at school which is too early so it takes ages to get to sleep. I only think about the next day if something bad is going to happen."

Escaping into a secret world can help, but these students were not always able to describe this very easily.

"I like to think I am air traffic controlling at Gatwick."

"I always go into a daydream land."

"I want to be in the Simpsons."

Parental support

In the main, parents are described as being very supportive, and students value their involvement in school matters.

"I like them coming into school because then they can help me."

There appear to be few occasions when they disagree, but when they do it is always over homework.

"They tell me that I have to do my homework when I don't want to."

"I disagree with my parents over how much work I have to do."

Sometimes lying is the only option!

"I say I have left my homework at home, but I've actually not done it."

Parents do have to be harsh at times.

"I don't like them talking to school because they often ground me."

"They can't understand why I don't like talking to new people."

A magic wand

Students were asked what one thing they would change if they had a magic wand.

"I would make it a happier place."

"Can we have more days off and half-terms?"

"I'd like more doing lessons and less writing."

"Change the timetable and have no PE."

"Ban homework and finish early every day."

And finally …

"I'd change the food. Bigger rations and a juicy steak!"

Some conclusions

Much of what has been written in this book is self-explanatory. It has come from the students themselves. It is not, therefore, bound up in jargon and difficult to understand.

Perhaps the main thing that comes across is the number of students in our schools who are bewildered and confused by the systems that surround them. Those that experience difficulties with their learning often spend their days wondering what is coming next and why they haven't got it right when others have. I hope I have been able to convey the sense of hopelessness that some of them feel.

Most were anxious to contribute, although many were nervous about putting their name to their comments. I have respected their wishes in every case. It is both their wish and mine that all who read this book will appreciate more fully the very real problems that exist for a sizeable proportion of students in our schools and colleges. Only then can some real changes take place, so that every student can find him or herself ready and able to learn in a helpful and supportive atmosphere.

It is interesting to see how consistent the comments are across the board on topics such as homework and reading aloud. It is generally assumed that students will dislike these areas of school life, without appreciating why. Here, we have the reasons spelt out and it is easier to feel empathy with students who are able to express themselves so forcibly. Hopefully, more teachers are beginning to think a little more creatively about the homework they set, to accommodate the different learning styles whilst appreciating the effort that some students have to put in to complete their work.

There are still some students who live in fear of their teachers, and some who have no real relationship with them. This does not help the learning process; it does not place the student in a receptive state for learning, and it cuts across the hierarchy of need set out by Maslow in the 1950's and still relevant today.

It is so important to appreciate the difficulties some students have, and not to punish them for something that is a clear manifestation of their learning disability.

The thing that surprises me still is the sheer resilience of many of the students we spoke to. Despite their problems, they emerge as determined young people, confident that some day all will be well. Even those who are stressed and who find school life really hard are still hanging in there and doing their best.

It is encouraging to see the support systems that are so vital to them increasingly in evidence. In addition, parents and friends play a significant role in supporting these students and helping them to realize their considerable potential. It is humbling to read the comments on the teachers who play their part in teaching the essential life skills. Their commitment and willingness to go the extra mile can literally turn someone's life around.

We owe it to these young people to listen to what they tell us, and to learn from them so that our schools become places where every student can feel valued with a sense of belonging. It is only then that we can be confident that our young people are all growing and learning as they should, whilst retaining their individuality.

My ideal school

My school was great, it had so many things right with it. Good support was always available and there were plenty of nice teachers, though of course none of us bothered to notice. We were all too busy complaining about the school dinners on Tuesdays (mushroom stroganoff is awful the first time but every Tuesday is it really necessary?).

Of course we were talking about the latest computer game because that's what made most of our school tick. I think however we all appreciated the support in some way.

There were however a few minor problems with the school, one was the severe lack of female activity (puberty with no girls and filtered Internet can be very depressing unless you find another way round it!). After that there is just the simple fact that none of us would accept our 'difficulties' and so spent all our time complaining about how lazy or stupid the other inhabitants were.

There was of course another route that could be taken and that was to bully or discriminate against each other. I was always affected by bullying even if it wasn't that bad. And do you know what they would always say to me to 'help'? They would say, 'ignore them'. I received that one piece of utterly useless advice for eleven years of my life. When you have such a poor level of tolerance as I do, with Asperger's syndrome and dyslexia, you will understand why I got so irritated.

Moving back to the subject of an ideal school because I was starting to ramble, I think a perfect school for children with 'difficulties' should have:

- mixed sexes with separate dorms just so pupils can develop socially as well as academically and so they don't get a big surprise when they get dumped straight into college and there is something there that wasn't before
- security cameras everywhere except the dorms to spot and stop bullying
- an interesting location – the hill at my school provided exercise and some of the students really need it, from what I've seen
- and of course the same devotion and support given by the teachers because that was great.

Thank you for this chance to say something as well as draw stickmen and I hope the book does well "cough cough".

Stuart Boyde – Illustrator
February 2004

If you enjoyed this book why not read ...

In Step with your Class
Managing Behaviour in an Inclusive Classroom
by Noel Janis-Norton

Valuable learning time can be wasted through behavioural issues. To maximise the strengths and minimise the problems of an atypical learner, this book addresses motivation, confidence, behaviour and basic skills.

- Practical advice to make classroom management easier and help pupils achieve their best.
- Written by a specialist with a wealth of experience training children, teachers and parents

ISBN 1-842992-17-1

You can order this book direct from:

Macmillan Distribution Ltd, Brunel Road, Houndmills, Basingstoke, Hampshire RG21 6XS

Tel 01256 302699

Email mdl@macmillan.co.uk